A D

I D

A

S

ALL DAY

I DREAM

ABOUT

SIRENS

DOMENICA MARTINELLO

COACH HOUSE BOOKS | TORONTO

first edition

 Canada Council   Conseil des Arts
for the Arts   du Canada

ONTARIO ARTS COUNCIL
CONSEIL DES ARTS DE L'ONTARIO
an Ontario government agency
un organisme du gouvernement de l'Ontario

 Canadä

Published with the generous assistance of the Canada Council for the
Arts and the Ontario Arts Council. Coach House Books also gratefully
acknowledges the support of the Government of Canada through the
Canada Book Fund and the Government of Ontario through the Ontario
Book Publishing Tax Credit.

LIBRARY AND ARCHIVES CANADA CATALOGUING IN PUBLICATION

Title: All day I dream about sirens / Domenica Martinello.
Names: Martinello Domenica, 1991- author.
Description: Poems.
Identifiers: Canadiana (print) 20190050489 | Canadiana (ebook)
20190050497 | ISBN 9781552453827 (softcover) | ISBN 9781770565890
(EPUB) | ISBN 9781770565906 (PDF)
Classification: LCC PS8626.A77445 A75 2019 | DDC C811/.6—dc23

All Day I Dream About Sirens is available as an ebook: ISBN 978 1 77056
589 0 (EPUB), ISBN 978 1 77056 590 6 (PDF).

To my family

TABLE OF CONTENTS

III. THIRD SPACE

O, MORNING COMMUTER

In the beginning there was in
corporation
       – it gets juicier, let's try

Seattle, 1971: pretty as a picture
of a seashell, burst forth from
the steaming, gently scalloped
fossil, belonging as easily

on the foamy beach as in a café
bathroom art motif – wait!
here, I've set aside the lyre.

This is a conduct story now.

I've taken up my new instrument.

             denuded full of secrets
        small smirk of oyster-like delight

Split-tailed sea cow, crowned.
Bird-brained *trompe l'oeil*: hi!
I've been drafted to perfection four times.
Designed to pull you in like a writhing net

but pleasantly. If a sixteenth-century Norse woodcut
forced someone in corporate to think
deeply on the
exciting
   seafaring

       history
          of coffee
anything can be mined for material.
Starbuck from Nantucket was a realist

though he wouldn't have minded a little navel.
Which was axed after my breasts. I was once
          quite Rubenesque

            currently nice   as a city   in france
            roundly singing in the romance tongues

– envision it now
as it's meant to be: a love story
in cropped body parts

          (can parts be
              symbols   sexed
              as in   sex symbol?
              as in   screen siren?

          Market research says:

                          yes!

      insert a call
      to action)

Learn more about your lack today. Claim
a third space, together outside of community
and solitude. My calling to forever sing you
the song of yourself: you
               are special

                              deserving of leisure
                    the lord decried this world
                              yours, of course, but also
                    a meritocracy and
                              guess what
                    yes
                              you still get premium access

the land owes you
its cream, spreads apart
yieldingly

          with no additional
          ads or fees.

Bespectacled bards, sight 20/20, re
visioned me in a crystal think tank.
That's where I live. We all get along swimmingly…

                              ah ah! – Watch my eyes.
                                        Stay with me.

I have a story   if you'd lend me
                          the rosy shell
                          of your ear.

I can see straight   into the
                          gaping
whole of your head   now.

Here's another version
of how this all goes.

I

HIGH NOON

Not a cruel song, no, no, not cruel at all. This song
is sweet. It is sweet. The heart dies of this sweetness.

– Brigit Pegeen Kelly

If ever there was a story without a shadow, it would be this: that
we as women exist in direct sunlight only.

– Terry Tempest Williams

ADIDAS

If you are the siren why do you balk at rebranding? A hot iron can turn a sea cow into iconography. Split-tailed, plucked smooth as a Brazilian wax. If you are the siren there's cognitive surplus, ennui, affluent sea of the net. If you are the siren you are freed from your circle, liberated from your outer ring into the great cabal of symbols. If you are the siren you're the Madonna of mermaids: about to ruffle some feathers. If you are the siren this isn't new. History-laden, a copywriter's muse. If you are the siren you are somebody's handmaiden, Persephone or Howard Schultz. Go forth toward the comments section. If you are the siren you are defined by an elite and wealthy heritage. Foamy Moby Dick boat cruise, milky sweet. Picked clean, bleached white. If you are the siren green your specific shade of green. If you are the siren create order, be beacon, be shimmering dyad palmed by the effete. If you are the siren you are at the forefront of the consumer revolution, sustainable and cruelty free. If you are the siren, over the last forty years we've made some changes to that identity. We sell entry to a community of like-minded people, cattle them in, strike at the pulsepoint of the sun. If you are the siren, you will do the rest.

Gnomon looming, shadow flatly dissecting body parts. Morning: I
struck out under past indiscretion. Afternoon: mouth, then neck
darkened by a hovering hand. Moves like a ripple, contemplating.

Divided, the sun's hot ceiling. Circling like a vulture, face making.
An unaligned zodiac, cleaved to inarticulacy. Evenings: I sore
and unassembled, singular mum shade. Moon does not gesticulate.

Stuck.

THIRTEEN WAYS TO OPTIMIZE YOUR
UNDERWATER BRAND

Mythology is rife with fishy women. *Mer* for matronly ocean,
maid for servitude in clamshells. From the brine came a perfectly
curvaceous specimen who swam her way through history
and splayed herself lavishly on the jutting rocks of our hearts.
Splicing sea monsters with airtight maidenhood has created
a staple in questionable storytelling from Ithaca to Denmark.
What do sirens and Ariel have in common? Tits, tunes, 'n' fins!
From fish-to fearmonger, here are some bewitching examples
of how various ages spawn a lolling trollop // animal pastiche
// high camp // niche // bestselling Barbie // rainbow titillation
// underage hair combing with a fork. Here's the aqueous,
the spume, acquiescent, dangerous
female logo.

PARTHENOPE

O, tactician
what great tact

you have while I
unshell my breasts

and sink, much
suffering stomach

churned lovesick
by avian flus.

My wetness
quenched Virgil,

quelled Vesuvius,
tears filled the sea

with pearls, voice
bleached the bones

my sisters cut
their teeth on.

Now humiliated
cities will be named

after me – me who's sick
for thighs and seaweed slick

for a thick old
bone like you,

a slit of wind taunting
ankles ankles ankles.

Foreman of men, you've
domesticated me.

Swallow a strand
of my long black hair

and we can call it
monogamy.

CATTLE OF THE SUN

my ex   once lived
in a house   later dubbed
the 'chattel ranch'

it wasn't   a ranch
when he lived there   though
his six starving roommates padlocked
their rooms   and the one

female roommate   padded around
marking their doors   in trickster
ink   drew dicks

and other epithets   to humiliate
them each time she got
drunk   she cocked her   sharpie
to stave off the   already gathering

smell   of hay

~

each room   a   padlocked
stanza   where the word *blue*
hasn't been invented yet

~

Ulysses made our bed
bought   the frame for cheap

it seemed   important to have
                 someone

to take   the long journey
to IKEA with

existing out of time   eyes an
indescribable *yes* of light   no language or
                    warning for it

∽

back at the ranch   the furies
provoke   slaughter
on the suitors
sliding down   the halls
barding   post-monogamous   stores of beer

like swine   they
won't   mix
wine with water   or wait
for a *yes*

yes hasn't been
invented yet

∽

hello!   my name is:
hard-to-translate
my doglike face
hounds men to make

collect calls
home   to their moms

boys will be boys
at the ranch
and launch a thousand ships
on your face

damn

that's one busy
                              refrain

one version goes   you're safe
one version goes   you're safe if
                              you sleep   in a marked doorway

smudged with hot girlish smoke   you can smell
her breath raging
like oxen   they say

⌣

the bedframe's in all the movies
sleep   and dream
a quiet   art
department's   budget

be recognized   forever
in cheap plainness

or die a bitch's death
in complex glory on the floor

~

each stanza has   an olive
tree growing   through it
not immovable   no
but laborious then to   extrapolate

REFRAIN ON THE ROCKS

Shipwrecked on the rocks (repeat ×3) Vernacular on the rocks
(end stop) Slick scales (repeat ×2) on the rocks (sharp breath)
Pinup sluts (release) on the rocks (pause) Coffee cups (hesitate)
on the rocks (end stop) Mixed feelings on the rocks (repeat
x2) Booze (repeat ×3) on the rocks (end stop) Water to wine
(pause) on the rocks (slow) Drowned body (slowly, hushed)
singing (ellipsis) on the rocks (end stop) Syllo (slowly, ellipsis)
gism (repeat slowly ×3)

MODEST GLITZ

Like a gold ring in a pig's snout is a beautiful woman without discretion. – Proverbs 11:22

maybe a fish never happens once and is finished

certainly if you bring the gun the gun comes back

certainly we've names and weapons licked in the envelope

certainly weave shrouds

maybe a bait

maybe a shamed

certainly a clue or a vow

maybe the velvet-grass breath of a sensitive cow

maybe a void the hot mammalian meat

maybe a void the hot human stomach

maybe the apple's a lemon an abattoir

certainly bodies break bread

certainly new conjugals

maybe her flaming jugs I mean tongues

maybe congrats on trying the devil's nail polish

maybe if you introduce a motive a motive sticks

certainly a swim's never swum once

certainly be gun not gash

maybe leak vinegar

maybe gall and myrrh today and forever

maybe a swipe of lipstick on these bristly boar lips

maybe jugular

certainly knives

MELUSINE

Filles du Roi // snatched by salt // and seaweed
their hopeful // Frenchness // transformed
into unspreadable // virgins // most horrible
to behold. // Thought to exist // with a rational soul
but a wriggling // brute-like body // of a visionary kind.
Nourished by sin // of Starbuck // they are destined
for suicide // unless they contract // a marriage
with a man // or read Joyce's // dirty love letters
without // giggling

BAIT SONG

siren – noisy vice mag – harpy – new tab – turn to weather –
suicide girl snip snip – tab tab – undine – iodine – nixie: nokken:
nicor: neck – blighted bra shells bite bite – nereids – twitter
deity – potamides – moisture-rich serum dab dab – limnad –
splash – oceanid – salt pill – scylla – ashrays – thirsty mermaid –
sob sob facial – rusalka – foppish – selkie – fop news –
charybdis – buzzardfeed – click click toilet – drippy drawl caw
caw – melusine – double double yummy please – make a zine –
makara – mockumentary – they're real! – milky milky koi –
caveat – yacuruna – yoni steam – fishy madams – jengu –
caviar – beach hair – wet dream pinterest – because you
watched: lady of the lake – lorelei – a lie a lie – two thighs –
two billion streams – dumpy dam leak – skip skip skip –
spotify – sigh – O sick! this ol' tune again –   λ

PRIVATE MYTHOLOGIES

1

teeth ache to cut the plates of your collarbones. mouth
craves mineral deposits, mauled marrow, the dizzy koan

of a stone beneath your tongue. skip rocks on my beach
before the tide recedes, the sand dries so quickly. bye, frogs.

bye, brown glass. things change,
how satisfying: the cellular gnash

a fossil beneath
the ancestral nail bed.

2

knead
the wrinkles

about your eyes
unage a decade

return to rubber
formative years

little white
pebbles for teeth

3

find

soft ancient coastline

in the crook of my arm

TARAXACUM

there are cracks
in my praxis
where Purdy's

yellow flowers
poke through
wear my working

class like a lion's
tooth its asexual
uniformed attire

milk rubber
genetically
identical

a common
man's odyssey
in a seed's blow

where ode
becomes episode
weeds grow

hopeful
can I get
some musical

accompaniment
here can I get
it in my wine

can I get it
in my salad
commonplace

and edible
like me
like me

please

REFRAIN ON THE ROCKS
after Apollinaire

In the end you've had it with technology
with all the passwords and floors

quarried from the same little cliffside in Florence

when attention to detail is a luxury
when aluminum or cotton is
when something is so new it looks old
it is a luxury too

that and plainspeak
when things are basic

who will act as chorus and will it be free

simple and streamlined
anodized or stonewashed

luxury in thread counts
in picking up threads
of time

to stop and listen
to the sound of the sea
made up

of an infinity of lesser sounds

sea I am like you
combed through with coloured glass

cicadas are so gentle and ugly do they have to be
the chorus

I guess if they rub loudly enough

I combed Lake Erie for fossils
picked a shoreline of moulted shells
that the grasses blew down to the beach
what does it mean

you in Florence with the fine-grained Pietra Serena sandstone

you in the motel on rue Saint-Denis

how can I reconcile my poverty

poetry of a janitor's daughter
with an iPhone and a degree

my grandmother cut off all her hair
so it wouldn't get caught in a factory machine

what luxury

to leap into the unknown to leap into water
to leap into the twisted skein to leap into sea
to leap into the mud to leap into silkweed
to leap into the future to leap through your screen

do you think you should be scuttling silently down there
do you think
do you
sing

cicadas like mythic land lobsters
they'll sing for you and everyone
if for Pliny and Homer and Tumblr
why not you

every birthday spent at Red Lobster was a luxury

have you had it

with buzzwords and epithets
the frothing i – i – i –

you with the proof in the rock and in the rock's pathetic pining

you pay your fare your fond farewell

let the sun bleach the floor

SINGSONG

All hail the man-made beach and
the man-made sand and the artisanal
sandwiches just out of reach of
my sunburnt hands fist deep in
that sweet neon pail of time
so plastic and toxically cheap.

II

ON THE ROCKS

When I first discovered in the early 1980s the Italian espresso bars in my trip to Italy, the vision was to recreate that for America – a third place that had not existed before.

– Howard Schultz

Her grandmother called the birds fishes, or the little mermaid would not have understood what was meant, for she had never seen birds.

– Hans Christian Andersen

ZENITH

11 a.m.

Come now. Take a crack at us.
Fish-women may be familiar

to you, or duplicitous women
doubling, working in twos.

11:30 a.m.

True, many men take a crack
but you don't strike us as someone

so easy to bruise. We explore conflict
through metaphor, isn't that true?

12 p.m.

Freud! what is your qualm with us?
Come. Join me. Join us on the rocks.

Jung, do you dream of swimming
or flying? I'm a cruelly numinous

12:15 p.m.

creature. I can accommodate. Memory
puddles like water, shimmers with heat,

≈ 38 ≈

changes colour on the hour. As a boy
did you dream of monsters in dark grottos

12:30 p.m.

who approach, threaten? We do not reproach.
Little fish, how do you break free of recurring

dreams when you're petrified, when we don
the face of your mother, her lullabies?

12:40 p.m.

The thing about lullabies: you're gone
before you hear their conclusion.

12:42 p.m.

Lie with us. There is no resolution.

SUMMER IN CAPRI

Holy water of the monastery
toilet water of the prison
swimhole of the rich.

There's less pressure
on your boats
and joints
if you float
you stupid
bobbing apples.

Hey Leucosia
Hey Ligeia
Hey Parthenope

what did you gals *really*
do to Marco Polo?

PARTHENOPE, EMBODIED

emboldened,
my black hair

grows back
… stranged.

let my razor
go dull as

sea glass.
stubble

scales me,
hot swarm

of ants
down my

belly, my
arms and hinges

wet brine
behind my

ear, a bone
dried out –

a moulted
thing with

feathers
and thick

viscous tar, a be
-witched spring

chicken at the farm.
what's your

one weird trick?
I've got two

or three.
put my body

on the block
and blow me

like a reed –
I can live

without a head
for months,

little crumb,
try me.

THE LAST SURVIVING SEA SILK SEAMSTRESS

1

God said, *Let there be byssus*,
and out sprouted the first blond
trees of Sorrento. We sun our hair
with lemon juice like bewitched algae
on the rocks, a golden embroidery
on the sea's harried lip. Attached
to Virgil's olive branch was a meaty
clump of seaweed the same swollen hue
as our nipples dripping oil, a time
                    before currency.

The line between sea
and seamstress is three
times finer than human
hair. We called each one
            seamistress,
pearls of saliva on a thread
1,000 years long, and soon

            an empty loom spun out.

2

God said, *Let there be math*,
and we soused King Solomon
clean of his robes – he was wicked
at the breaststroke. Each boat
a little blot of treachery, so willing

to singe the sea with bleach. Whenever
we need a bone to pick our teeth, we sing
our throats into a moneyed tinkle
and a toothpick comes rowing.
Heads as hard as coins licked
green with salt and mouldering,
our hair a darkening oil slick,
fungal seafloor, smouldering.

Have you ever tried
to profit from the tides?
It's now almost impossible
to coax myths from the blue
patterned fabric of the world.

Its lustre clogged with plastic,
backlit. Already dim human
eyes weakening like a filament
disappearing into a silk seam.

3

God said, *Thoughts and prayers for this awful tragedy*,
everything's quick and bald in the twenty-first century.
The sun hangs in the sky like a logo
and we lose our honeyed fleece,
black and falling out in fistfuls.

Forehead bowed at the precipice, the fingers
of the last *seamistress* slowly succumb
to chalkstone, barren. The rocks grow dark
and slick at the thought: there's no one left

to swear in. No kin or skein or women
to weave after her daughter's refusal
of the thread between her teeth:
                oaths and patience
                and a tolerance
                for mystery,
the ocean's true productivity
turns skulls to coral reef.

Every man
adores a casket

if it's lush and lined,
dyed seaweed green,
the cost of every shipwreck
rubbing up against
our spleen.

4

God said, *I am dead*,
gout and the museums killed me.
The last surviving sea silk seamstress
opens her door for free.

MERCY MERCY

> *But when you pray, use not vain repetitions, as the heathen*
> *do: for they think that they shall be heard for their much*
> *speaking.* – Matthew 6:7

Thank god for days dreaded they last forever

Thank god for the fact of your skin

Thank god you didn't crush the scent out

What a blessing to be kept all night by a body so true

Thank god for the midnight sprinkler timer true as dogs

Thank god for fingers more or less

Thank god for the boulder rolled away from my opening

Thank god for your hung collarbones

What a blessing the death control pills

What a blessing grass lurid after heavy rain

What a blessing Pavlov

Thank god I'm dumb

Thank god I'm drooling

Thank god for sexless flowering

What a blessing to be a cold orchid

Thank god the cube melts slow

Thank god for implements to spruce the wilting

Thank god for the capacity to lie

Thank god it is truly a blessing

What a blessing to be broken and showing

ICHTHYS

foreshadowing jesus

jesus foreshow

a deluge of mermaid fanaticism

sources credit

multiplying

proto-eucharist

feeds the starving

gossip

breadbox

bready box

of gossiping

fishfood

indeed christianity

revered crowd-pleasing

edible symbols

his miracle

several mermaids

clutching the fine arches

loving handmaidens

of christ's feet

psalms

on crutches

step stones

cunning aquatic stroll

that strut tut tut

mary rumour

magdalen rumour

mermaid magdalen

villagers stoned

unwed wrists tied

bible sacrifice

imbibe

merlot magdalen

marred seafloor mary

weighty ritual

disintegrating

under the soles

in the gallery

of galilee

MIRACULOUS CATCH

maid of many bloods
and a cut through the middle

of me, half underscore
half sardine

skyline of two
hues clamping shut

~

all deceit
cannot be entered

cannot be entered
girded against

net and fishhook
loins of the mind

gaping quietly
a slow suggestive 'o'

~

composite of spring
matter, meat, and stones

attached by two fleshes
soul skewered to an arrow

stay deep, stay low
dark little baskets

darting in the shallows
multiply, starving

my soul too
thin to be collected

under the high gallery
and stained glass

of voiceful
wetness

⁓

men of many men
ready to accept

their new vocation
new ultimate tongue

grow their hair long
and useful

casting lines, weaving
creels from their beards

thinking the shoreline
is their shoreline, singular

sure the skyline
will crack open

like a walnut
if they will it

they will not get
their sandals wet

thinking they alone
can walk

that salty crease

THE FISH

If a man caught the fish
in Elizabeth Bishop's
'The Fish,' the man
would not have set
the fish free
in the end.

MILKSONG

Sorry to burst thru your lyric sully
tude but I'll procreate any moment.
Isn't anything looking like sperm sex
you all harkening back to your hot tad
pole days random erections, whatever
it's too bad when we grow out of our tails
into the poisonous frog army O
vary your rubdowns: still going to die
late like a hallway in heat sweaty pour
no mommy fluids aboard this aircraft.
Warty vixen maidens: consume thy mom
my poem's pornographic docu-cult –
This is not very modern anymore.
(Please delete your cervix.)

SAUCEBOX

Lucia is the first of Joyce's sirens.
– Carol Loeb Shloss

one's identity is hard-won
in language of household

and letterwriting, of leaving

and leaving

it is surely the most italian of activities
to be in love with charlie chaplin
yes I wanted forms of splendour

anti-mother tongued
trampin my way round dublin

⁓

from trieste to northampton it's exhausting
still basking
in my debt to you

why should a debtor's daughter pay
into a shoddy pocket

for a not-yet-determined
amount of his genius

yes I know yes
little match girl
wants legs

better to evade

～

six hrs a day age twenty-two
when I was ten how disorderly

how cross-eyed and evicted

and poor yes I cried for a month
drawing your lettrines

at ten I could have been illuminating
instead of thirteen in three countries

book of kells
broken at the prim shining bar

your and my blindness

straightjacket a stage
prop like any other body

bastardry

～

beckett's grouchiness
would drive anyone
to a complex

his majesty's
sour money strapped my legs for a
not-yet-determined stay
at the maison de santé

thanks sam

sorry I wasn't into condoms

it must be the pleasure-seeking
italian lesbian in me

write me

〜

little loony debt
for papa's fête

a chair against the wall
like the real artist

bra-lined bravado
coveting giorgio's

breast milk

illiterate in three languages
look what I can do

wave my arms
throw myself like a voice

about the room

⁓

yr blind I snip the phonelines

yr blind I snip the phonelines

fat with congrats I circumcise

unbutton your trousers *genius*

raked together a wake for me

restless kin yes it's complicated

we're illiterate in all languages

they missed their invite

but a real dancer makes do

UNLETTERED

after Domenica Martiniello (1932–2015)

Clutched my braid,
umbilical,

stashed in my pocket
like the small things

I'd steal from the grocery.
In Canada I realize

for the first time:
my name

is two crossed lines
on a cheque.

My hands make
and unmake everything,

X sharp as shearing scissors.
At least I don't need it

to pay cash
or scratch tickets.

At least a machine
won't scalp me.

〜

Granddaughter, we
don't all have the eye

to catch mistakes. We
weren't all swaddled

in newsprint
or schoolbooks.

My study hall
was a cowshed,

and later,
a bingo hall.

Later still
my memory

will go along
with my body

and all you'll have
is the silent *i*,

a rope fastened through
each one of your stories.

—

I never kissed
a picture of Mussolini.

I've kissed no one
but my husband.

He was happy peeling
potatoes in the army.

I bore children, worked
the fields, never seen

a soft elbow. Where
have you gone

and inherited those? It's
unbiblical. But your breasts

are my doing, useful
until neighbours put

the *malocchio* on you.
You'll get as many guests

as you do headaches and
the cows will miscarry.

⁓

Home was verbal, Naples
a verb. Volcano, courtyards

full of basil. In the gut
of my first winter

I imagined picking cherries,
chestnuts, and fennel

to brace against
the icy strangeness

of vowels
grinding metal,

threat of bony fingers nicked
down clean to the knuckle.

Strangers came
with cold hands.

I gave them zucchini
blossoms I froze

on the clothesline.
I thought: if I slip

and fall on the ice
who will go to work?

They'll replace me
with a Greek.

⁓

Your grandfather was happy
to clean floors

and so your father
cleaned floors, too.

Spent entire lifetimes
in school just like you.

We found money
on the ground back then,

eyes turned down
to our shoes.

How do you even look
people in the eye?

Your hair all cropped
and purposely mangled

like a perfumed boy.
I pray for my braid,

a severed offering,
the *i* missing

from your name.
A chain of ancestors

lined up in hot grasses
just to pass it to you.

One day you'll see
our name on a tombstone –

it's already happened –
the shame of your error

crossing you, a strike
from both sides.

Domenica, Sunday
of my Sunday –

why haven't you gone
and lettered the world with it?

ANATOMICAL MACHINES
Capella Sansevero, Naples

What is a body
but a bone bole
rewired beeswax
hot iron and silk

What is a bowl
of waxed fruit
painted lovingly
by scalpel stroke

Double moon peering
through the gnarled trellis
of a womanly bough

Two black basins
in a clean skull bend
the blood as it hardens

every path
is the centre
of an autopsy

to the heart
the viscera
is a system

mounted pedestal or plinth
fetus at her feet at some point

lower legs teeth one testicle
missing from the specimen

curious furniture

wax cabinet   ghastly ossein

thank alchemy

peace adam

piece eve

REFRAIN ON THE ROCKS

Mermaids drunk on limoncello. Sirens wag their tails as Sorrento's sacked by the Turks. Mermaids in aquamarine blue lipstick and bindis and vegan hair dye. Sirens wailing at the sails as a fleet of nimble ships sink. AquaMermaid classes rock the suburbs, 'It's all about the tail, fitness- and fantasy-wise.' Sirens screech and flail, looking rather male in the face, decides Columbus. Mermaids in sequined pushup bras really into burlesque. 'It's a big fin, so you push a lot of water.' Sirens warbling sailors toward the rocks, picking their teeth in a heap of soft boy bones. Mermaids with rockin' abdominals, killer core strength, arms like Venus Williams. From your boat or screen, the cliffs change colour every hour on the hour. Neat or on the rocks, someone's going to sink.

SAND

it takes millions of us

to make the world soft

III

THIRD SPACE

In almost every musical ever written, there's a place that's usually the third song of the evening, sometimes it's the second, sometimes it's the fourth ... the leading lady sits down on something and sings about what she wants in life and the audience falls in love with her and then roots for her to get it for the rest of the night.

– Howard Ashman

Though she's often referred to as a 'mermaid,' the Starbucks' Siren is technically more like a melusine – she's got a split tail. (Thereby solving the most vexing problem with mermaids ... Namely, how do you have sex with a fish-woman with no crotch?)

– Slate

PARTHENOPE AND VIRGIL

Women are cities and cities
are humiliating.

Tourists haggle the price
and somehow still pay double.

The city is leaky
and smells like fishwives.

Locals chide in dialect
tangy as a faux leather belt.

Men are angry and angry men
turn each other into volcanoes.

What is it like to live
in the shadow of a volcano?

On the cusp of eruption
it's exciting

for the tourists. Burning through
their cash, it's all you can smell.

Volcanoes violate cities
to ash and stone. It's a pity.

I'd pumice my feet with it all
if I could.

REFRAIN ON THE ROCKS
after Emily Wilson

mouths   not lips
knowledge   not wisdom

mouths not   lips know
ledge   not wisdom

lip of a mouth
a knowing ledge

    knotted   cog
    native naught

        moth   slips the knot
        waxing   cognation

mouths myth: lips know: was done

not: wooden   woo them
      femdom   with sibilant
      nation   lips mouthing
      math   mouthing
      sibilant math   no mast

make sibilant lips
a mouth of waxdom

                    unbunged.

JUICY CRONE

I wash out the scones in the world of money

     Scones in the grout of the coffee and sugar machines

The middle class million burnt up and shovelled

   Policing refills of half-and-half cream   I cash out

The local landfill

  Fulfill my prophecy

    Scrub the books scot-free

  Landfall

Purveyor of the patisserie

  Two-for-one stock split

Go passionately   to the seafaring place

I supplicate   chief executor

I reinforce   company policy

    French pressed in the second wave

I ring out mini demi   semi skim

Organize twin radical faith between brews

Wage the living war

I grow scones twice thrice my size grande   venti   trenta

Grinding the wheels of the last landlord

Satisfying grout machine with cold drink

I rub my scone in olive oil   and bring it to the notary

New non-citizens   abandoned in the break room

Cup an ear to your landform

Bodies of the frontline employees

Rowing

Spreading

Furiously useful

Exchanging of handicrafts   in domestic partnership

Spurned

Buttery minimum

Waging   the work

I work   to get there first   .   .   .

HAPAX SONG

I cut down all the wind chimes when you tell me

       Myth is everyone's favourite

Beach House song. What do you know

       about ethereal? About being startled

like a drawer of dropped forks? Granular whimsy.

       I shred my clothes and make a zine.

My flowers are Georgia O'Keeffes.

       When I cry it sounds like a scream

gliding through a beaded doorway.

       Before you dipped, I made a beach

by hand. Crushed cicada shells by moony

       pestle, slipped off the bank

like nude descending a staircase. The sand, all DIY,

singing: Frank's everyone's favourite, too.

DISNEY SONG

Little sister / seventh sister
Daddy named us well
// mollusk-soft daughters
for a great barrel-chested
bell /// We don't chime in
unless someone points
a stick at us //// Conductor
of daughters, of pearly white
belles ///// An empty shell is no
way to pander ////// to your
pitchfork Daddy's rancour.
Sing, sing so the audience
learns to forgive our Daddy
/////// his anger.

Seventh sister wants to run
her tongue over all her stuff
until it's dry as sandpaper
in the sun. Wants upward
mobility, hungers for a tan.
Daughters at the top don't get
reprimanded, wear smart suits,
lean in, suck their man's ten
wiggling toes of progress.
Want – uglier through repetition
like the world. Let's forgive her
cavern of treasures. Seventh sister
is the American Dream's
premium antiques collector.

it's the renaissance
of self-loathing
a fishbowl's the luckiest
tableware w/ the soft silt floor
that's the daughterly spot
why make a muck
of all the clean bubbles
why covet breakfast bread
aren't you lucky you're allowed
that wet knife
extra pinched waist
oscar-worthy calypso tease
sister there are worse fates
no fish jokes please

seventh sister, have you considered
a career in sea witchery or drag?
have you considered more literal
hunger more villainous curves? ~
have you considered the pleasures
of big women and skinny men?
have you considered, seventh sister
the magnificent creative powers
of repeating yourself over and over ~
have you considered death, seventh sister
or have you considered silence
in our glorious post-lyric age?
I haven't, for seventh sister, I own the ocean
it was born from my tit sweat ~

Something for tempting the palate
prepared in the classic technique: *Soleil
cou coupé* with a lemon and a succulent
crab up my sleeve. Pots clank on their pegs
in a mad kitchen slapstick, crass and happy
like the cleaving box of knives beneath
my apron. Surely you've never tasted
a bouillabaisse like it, *chéri*. Every scrap
fat and pregnant with mercury, butter
and flower as decried by *ce monde ancien*.
Alors, what's the word for rubbing yourself
with a mallet? The recipe calls for
pounding salt into my tender *bleu
sacré coeur,* so to speak, *Adieu*

I want   I want   I want
I want   I want   I want
I'm want   I'm want   I'm want
I'm what   I want   Wont to want
Want   Want   Want
Want   Wont   To want
I want I want I want I want I wet
Want
Want
Want   Wet
Want
What I want
Won't
I

PRIVATE MYTHOLOGIES

1

ancestral bedrock. collarbones dangling, euphoric fandom.

go. hit it. juicy kneading / lumbering

movements. no oracle pressing quiet rendezvous.

so titular. unassuming vestibule. waning x-rated youth,

zipped.

2

abacus beads cast down.   (*bye, beads*)

each father goes hovering in,

justifying. kingdoms lasting moments

nailed on placards. question

relations.

some toothache. uselessly viable wrinkles.
          /teething   whipper/snapper

Xanax Xanax Xanax Xanax Xmas Xanax Xanax,

yesterday's
          zag.

3

my alphabet's
never transcended
this stupid song and dance.

DEMETER'S HIVES

I cover myself in bees, attract an infinite swarm to my body,
living suit of armour. This I accomplish in under forty minutes.
My new skin smells animal, one hundred pounds
of honeyed warmth.

Wasp venom is the new cure for HIV but I hear bee stings
will cure you of sex altogether.

With my openings plugged, drones work themselves to death.

A swarm of swans could never be as graceful as a million points
of fat buzzing energy. Mum my nerves and soften to demonstrate
my insect rapport as the bees beard me genderless.

I don't know if you know this but swans are notoriously violent.

I never feel the need to sow myself anymore. Ever-pollinated,
my stomach's been tracked over and planted by tiny colonies.
The tickle and sting of it, a sensational extension of old news.

Now I ooze like milkweed from all my little cuts.
My womb is a nested catacomb, batted at with a broom.

Boatkeeper, washerwoman, Woman of Bruised Knees.
Now I'm honeyfarmer, Queenbreeder. Take me
into your arms. I speak the new language.

I don't know if you've heard but
I have a needle for a tongue.

CIRCE ON SUNDAYS

Circe watches some shade of herself played in a little glowing box. *Hades by any other name*, she thinks of HBO. Seasons change: One, two, three, four, five, six, lucky seven – she survives them all. Survives weatherless winters and exile to Italy and a house all confused, misruled. Misquoted as a nymph, witch, sorceress with a complex, name misspelled. She yells at the box and the box gives her a peek at next week. Her life does feel very episodic lately, a tactician's pit stop. The shades dip into their cups like gods and Circe thinks, *how realistic*. The beheadings are rather nice. She does not regret ending her husband's life and neither does her conniving blond double; for this she will not curse her to life as an actual lion. At one point her head is sheared and Circe finds this form of violent non-violence distasteful, ghost limb of hair lisping in silence. Somewhere a producer is turned into a dog. Despite the discrepancies, in truth it's nice for Circe to hear the sound of her name again. Howls make for a solitary island. She ups the volume, wraps her furs tighter. A man once said her bed was a dalliance, that she got stuck like a tack in his head. To hell with him. A year grows fat as she waits to hear her word again.

HOWARD SONG

Howard's stern Howard's wayward
son to many ward to none that wonderful
soothsaying Howard we all have one
rebrand holy tablets to Honour Thy Howard
in all His glory refusing handshakes on cable TV
that's our Howie! myriad Howards quirky lovable
hard-to-please Howard he's handmade in Brooklyn
extra quotable business acumen our hard-won Howard
the hard-ons in our hearts whispering   *hey hi*
we yearn for new names which Howard's apostles
write in Sharpie we appreciate all variations Howard
we are the history of Howard's hands we dream Howard's
dreams in Technicolor which Howard invented
or invested in we forget which Howard   did which

O JAMESY

yes yes I say Yes[1] calypso and liver aeolus and wind he smoked Pall Malls out the window and shivered epic of the body[2] I climbed out onto the fire escape in my slippers in my pink underwear in his long-sleeved shirt without a bra a scent unweaving tobacco sweetmeat cologne blood pudding deodorant a coded map in the fabric controlling each breath and stalling.[3] my speech began to imitate the rhythms of the printing press. his mouth found biting other mouths foreign[4] but soon grew accustomed to the dialect.[5] perhaps we're more sensitive to things surrounded by a sea of noise. moments slippery. hard to stack – epic of bodily juices epic of various wetnesses[6] – is it not that language is fluid[7] but that prose is a chamber pot[8]?

---

[1] He got into my taxi: the darkness, the rain, the fogged windows, an odyssey, a garrison.

[2] Beard hair soft. Pubic hair soft, untamed. Narrow shoulders wisped with single countable hairs. Ears little hairless shells.

[3] His eyes were a bovine hazel and I was the first person in the world to describe them; he said my smile lit up my face and all I smelt was burnt hair.

[4] Later our eyes met and bounced quickly off each other like two rubber balls.

[5] iloveyouiloveyounoyoudon'tyoudon'tknowmeifeelyouit'sagoodstorystop talkingsomuchjustgowithitwhatisloveislovecomfort?windbagwindbagwind baghereismybagofwind

[6] 'Water closet' sounds poetic and surreal, the deodorizing value of a turning a good phrase.

[7] *Joyce's Ulysses: A Reader's Guide* by Sean Sheehan assures me: Virginia Woolf and Bob Dylan have lost their way, too.

[8] Poetry as chamber music.

NEW NO MORE

no more mastheads
no more gatekeepers
no more birthing
spontaneously from heads
new heads
new blood
new ripe glorious
failure
no more tales
no more erecting
of monuments
no more mass
or amassing
no more taxes
no more keeping
or owning
new holding
new myths
new syntax
no more fallacy
no more tied to masts
no more wilful waxing
of ears, lyrical, sentimental
new feelings
no seals
no new extinctions
no more news
no sediment
no new innovations
without new stakes

through the heart
of new empathy
no more concepts
no more dis
embodiment
no more tills
or tenders
new nouns
new softness
new storytelling
new epics
no rulers
new rules
so newly familiar
until tenderness
is new
yes new
a new kind
that no one
can ever take
away from us.

VIRGINIA'S MOTH

My body's known poets, a legion of murmuring men.
Saying things like, *there's a whole narrative here*
while stumbling down the buttons of a blouse
twining hair in their fists and then suddenly
jerking back. Exposed jawline, faux tenderness
   sniffed and followed like a sentence.

My limbs have known Bukowskis, drunk and smoking cloves.
Staring casually at my body thinking, *no story here but movement.*
This, while I practically glisten in stasis under the heft
of their swagger. Muscles dimmed and dampened
by articulate fingers fixing me
   in glib oil.

My torso has known weight, has been pricked, pinned
down, hung off the edges of tables and beds, blushes
and vertigos have been sampled in attempted accuracy
transcribing my body's blood. Testing phrases, my breasts
have made for magnificent
   palate cleansers.

My heart's known nothing, is spotless, save for a cliché
of eyelids when things like, *I could craft long poems of your legs*
have been uttered. Like a murder of moths on the sill, still I refuse
their nocturnal net. Like a mishandled mythology skewered
shadowless on a bedpost, still I trail
   my stubborn dust.

REFRAIN ON THE ROCKS
after Robert Creeley

There is no happiness
wet or decent enough.

NOTES

'O, Morning Commuter,' p. 9: Founded in Seattle in 1971, Starbucks has redesigned its famous siren logo four times. The revisions have edited out parts of the siren's breasts, torso, arms, and tail. This poem is voiced by the Starbucks logo as she undergoes each redraft, testing out her new tactics, complete with several choral asides.

'Parthenope,' p. 17: In the Greek version of the siren myth, Parthenope fails to lure Odysseus with her song in Homer's *The Odyssey* (Odysseus has been warned by the goddess Circe to bung his ears up with wax and tie himself to the mast of his ship). Parthenope then drowns herself.

'Taraxacum,' p. 30: A scientific classification more commonly known as 'dandelion.'

'Refrain on the Rocks,' p. 32: The second 'Refrain on the Rocks' models itself after the poem 'Zone' by Guillaume Apollinaire (specifically David Lehman's translation). It also references 'The Love Song of J. Alfred Prufrock' by T. S. Eliot.

'The Last Surviving Sea Silk Seamstress,' p. 43: This poem is dedicated to Chiara Vigo, the last surviving sea silk seamstress. The poem, which shares its title with a very informative BBC article, reimagines sea silk fibres (byssus) as siren hair.

'Miraculous Catch,' p. 51: Inspired by the Bible story 'The Miraculous Catch of Fish' (Luke 5:1–11), this poem conflates details of several of Jesus's wet and fishy miracles.

'Saucebox,' p. 56: This poem is after Lucia Joyce. I make use of biographical details and anecdotal situations from Carol Loeb Shloss's *Lucia Joyce: To Dance in the Wake*.

'Anatomical Machines,' p. 66: Two eighteenth-century anatomical models ('Adam' and 'Eve'), referred to as Anatomical Machines, are on display in a chapel in Naples. Because the circulatory system is so convincingly reproduced on top of their human skeletons, it was believed that Adam and Eve were injected with an alchemical substance that hardened their blood while still alive. This occult theory has since been debunked.

Due to pelvic fractures, the female anatomical model is suspected to have died in childbirth, and a preserved fetus was placed at her feet. The fetus was stolen in the 1990s and never recovered.

'Refrain on the Rocks,' p. 70: The third 'Refrain on the Rocks' cribs lines from an article titled 'Mermaid school opens in Montreal – but who's taking the plunge?' by Amanda Kelly for Global News.

'Parthenope and Virgil,' p. 74: In the Roman version of the siren myth, Parthenope incurs Jupiter's jealous wrath by taking a lover. As punishment, he transforms them into physical landforms: Parthenope becomes the city of Naples and her lover, the angry volcano Vesuvius.

'Refrain on the Rocks,' p. 75: The fourth 'Refrain on the Rocks' references a Twitter thread by Emily Wilson on her new translation of *The Odyssey*. Wilson examines specific liberties taken by male translators when it comes to sexualizing the sirens, such as adding in descriptions of their hair and consistently mistranslating the word 'mouth' as 'lips' and 'knowledge' as 'wisdom.'

@EmilyRCWilson: 'The Sirens in Homer aren't sexy… The seduction they offer is cognitive: they claim to know everything about the war in Troy, and everything on earth. They tell the names of pain.' (4 March 2018, 4:12 p.m. Tweet.)

'Disney Song,' p. 80: Each section of 'Disney Song' is, chronologically, based on a song from *The Little Mermaid*, composed by Howard Ashman: 'Daughters of Triton,' 'A Whole New World,' 'Under the Sea,' 'Poor Unfortunate Souls,' 'Les Poissons,' and 'Kiss the Girl.' The fifth section riffs, again, on 'Zone' by Guillaume Apollinaire.

'Circe on Sundays,' p. 89: The goddess Circe is in conversation with Cersei Lannister of *Game of Thrones*.

'O Jamesy,' p. 91: The title of 'O Jamesy' refers to a moment in the last chapter of *Ulysses* when Molly Bloom seemingly addresses Joyce directly: 'O Jamesy let me up out of this pooh.'

'Refrain on the Rocks,' p. 95: The last 'Refrain on the Rocks' is in response to Robert Creeley's 'The Rain.'

ACKNOWLEDGEMENTS

Thank you to my family, particularly to my parents, Lynn Gervais and Frank Martiniello, as well as Chantal Fortier, Maria Salerno, Mario Visconti, and Franca Visconti. To my wonderful partner, Gino Visconti, thank you for your love, support, and life-giving laughter. To my chosen siblings, Samantha Katharine, Greg Mattigetz, Ashley Olivieri, and Catherine Scarpone, thank you for making so many cycles of life less lonely.

To the Canada Council for the Arts, who provided financial support during the crucial beginning stages of this project: thank you for investing in me so early.

Gratitude to the editors of the following publications for publishing versions of these poems: *carte blanche, Contemporary Verse 2, Cosmonauts Avenue*, DUSIE blog, *Lemon Hound*, NewPoetry.ca, *PRISM International, The Puritan,* and *THIS Magazine.*

Thank you to the Writers' Trust of Canada, Carolyn Smart, and judges Adéle Barclay, Stuart Ross, and Moez Surani for nominating a selection from *All Day I Dream About Sirens* for the Bronwen Wallace Award for Emerging Writers in 2017. The ten selected poems were also published as an iBook.

To my talented and loving friends and peers in Montréal, Toronto, and Iowa City: I am so lucky to know you. Please feel my awe and appreciation always.

My admiration and gratitude for the mentorship and guidance of Stephanie Bolster, Suzanne Buffam, Jim Galvin, Spencer Gordon, Susan Holbrook, Matthea Harvey, Michael Holmes,

Stevie Howell, Andrew Katz, Mark Levine, Jane Mead, Alex Porco, Sina Queyras, Rudrapriya Rathore, Jessica Rattray, Robyn Schiff, Alana Wilcox, Elizabeth Willis, and Catriona Wright, among so many others.

This project would not have been possible without the encouragement and support of Jay and Hazel Millar.

Domenica Martinello is a writer from Montréal, Quebec. She was a finalist for the 2017 Bronwen Wallace Award for Emerging Writers and holds an MFA in poetry from the Iowa Writers' Workshop, where she was the recipient of the Deena Davidson Friedman Prize for Poetry. *All Day I Dream About Sirens* is her first book.

Typeset in Arno and Gotham

Printed at the Coach House on bpNichol Lane in Toronto,
Ontario, on Zephyr Antique Laid paper, which was manufac-
tured, acid-free, in Saint-Jérôme, Quebec, from second-growth
forests. This book was printed with vegetable-based ink on a
1973 Heidelberg KORD offset litho press. Its pages were folded
on a Baumfolder, gathered by hand, bound on a Sulby Auto-
Minabinda, and trimmed on a Polar single-knife cutter.

Edited by Susan Holbrook
Designed by Crystal Sikma
Cover art 'Punishment of the Envious' by Guy Marchant
Author photo by Abdul Malik

Coach House Books
80 bpNichol Lane
Toronto ON M5S 3J4
Canada

416 979 2217
800 367 6360

mail@chbooks.com
www.chbooks.com